Without great solitude, No serious work is possible.

Albert Einstein

"When the going gets tough,
the tough get going."

– Joe Kennedy

"It does not matter
how slowly you go
as long as you do not stop. "

–Confucius

"Without great solitude,
No serious work is possible."

– Albert Einstein

"To accomplish great things,
we must not only act,
but also dream,
not only plan, but also believe."

– Anatole France.

"Opportunities don't happen,
you create them."

– Chris Grosser.

"Good, better, best.
Never let it rest.
'Til
your good is better
and your better is best."
– **St. Jerome**

"Optimism is the faith
that leads to achievement.
Nothing can be done without
hope and confidence."

– Helen Keller

"Live as if you were
to die tomorrow.
Learn as if you were
to live forever."

– Mahatma Gandhi

"That which does not kill us makes us stronger."

– Friedrich Nietzsche

"Be who you are and say
what you feel,
because those who mind
don't matter and those who
matter don't mind."

– Bernard M. Baruch

"We must not allow
other people's
limited perceptions
to define us."

– Virginia Satir

"Do what you can,
with what you have,
where you are."

– Theodore Roosevelt

It's not bragging
if you can
back it up."

– Muhammad Ali

"Be yourself; everyone else
is already taken."

– Oscar Wilde

"This above all:
to think
own self be true."

– William Shakespeare

"If you cannot do great things,
do small things in a great way."

– Napoleon Hill

> "If opportunity doesn't knock,
> build a door."
>
> **– Milton Berle**

"Wise men speak because they
have something to say;
fools because they have
to say something."
– Plato

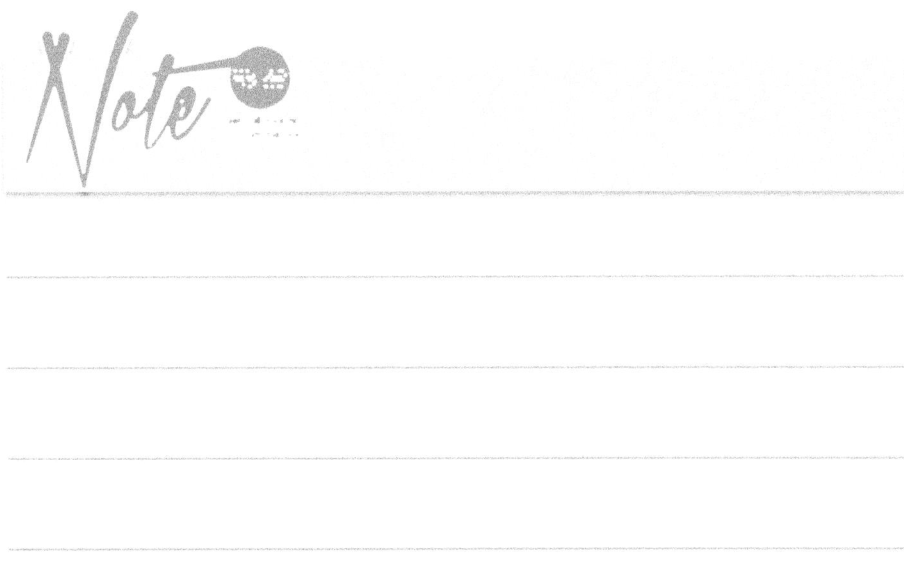

"Strive not to be a success,
but rather to be of value."

– Albert Einstein

"Two roads diverged in a wood, and I—I took the one less traveled by, And that has made all the difference."
– Robert Frost

"Do not let what
you cannot do interfere with
what you can do."

– John Wooden

"Whenever you find yourself
on the side of the majority,
it is time to pause
and reflect."

– Mark Twain

"I haven't failed.
I've just found 10,000 ways
that won't work."

– Thomas Edison

"A journey of a thousand leagues begins beneath one's feet."

– Lao Tzu

"I've learned that people will forget what you said, people will forget what you did, but people will never forget how you made them feel."

– Maya Angelou

"Either you run the day,
or the day runs you."

– Jim Rohn

"Life shrinks or expands in proportion to one's courage."

– Anais Nin

"You must be the change you wish to see in the world."

– Mahatma Gandhi

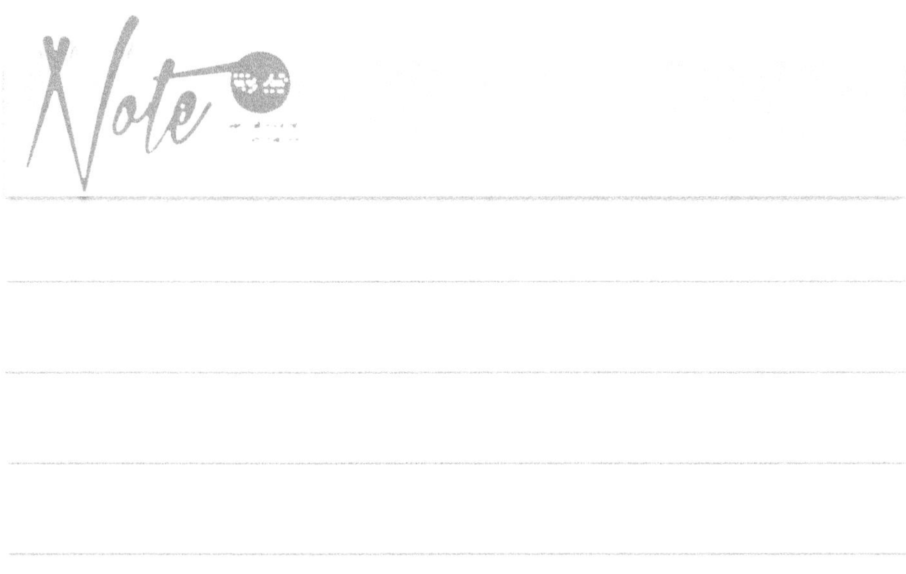

"What you do speaks so loudly that I cannot hear what you say."

– Ralph Waldo Emerson

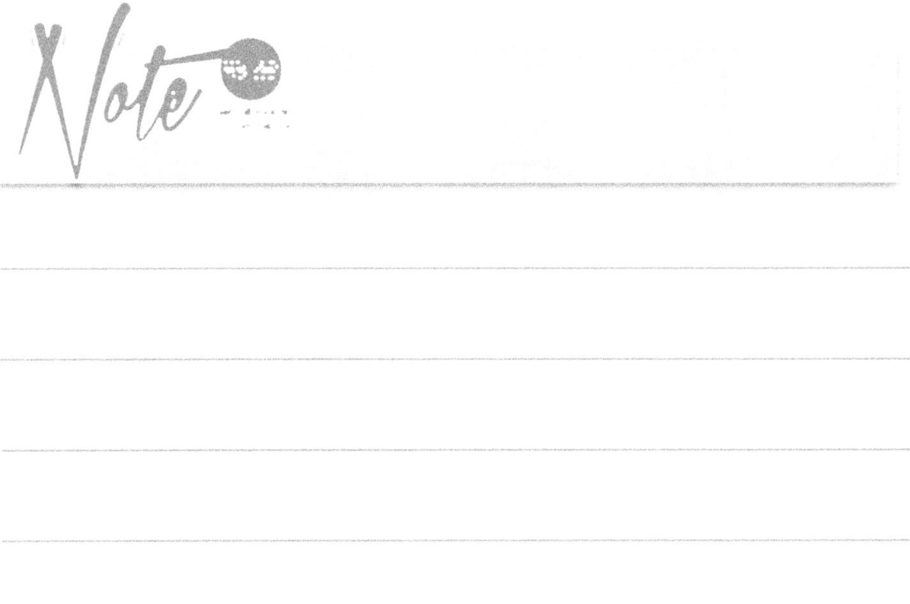

"Believe and act as if it were impossible to fail."

– Charles Kettering

Quote

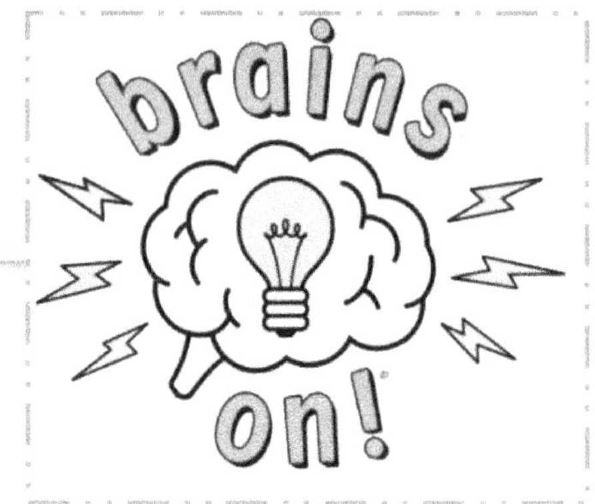

"The difference between ordinary and extraordinary is that little extra."

– Jimmy Johnson

Note

"The best way to predict
the future is to invent it."

– Alan Kay

"If I am not for myself,
who is for me?
And if I am only for myself,
what am I?
And if not now, when?"

– Rabbi Hillel

"Everything has beauty,
but not everyone can see."

– Confucius

"Believe you can and you're halfway there."

– Theodore Roosevelt

"How wonderful it is that nobody need wait a single moment before starting to improve the world."

– Anne Frank

"Imagination is everything.
It is the preview
of life's coming attractions."

– Albert Einstein

"Change your thoughts
and you change your world."

– Norman Vincent

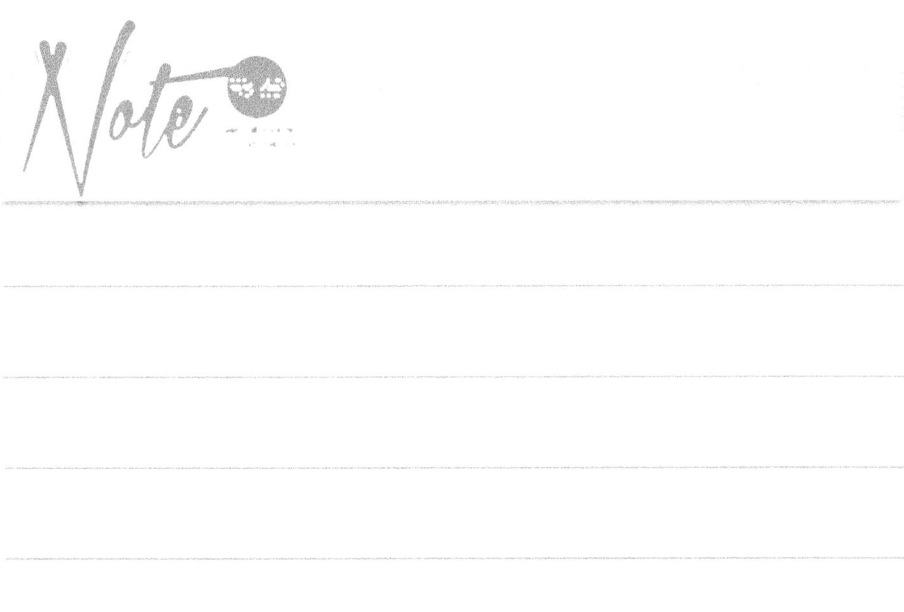

"Happiness is not something ready made.
It comes from your own actions."

– Dalai Lama

"Remember that happiness
is a way of travel,
not a destination."

– Roy M. Goodman

Too many of us are not living
our dreams because
we are living our fears."

– Les Brown

"If you want to lift yourself up,
lift up someone else."

– Booker T. Washington

"You miss 100% of the shots
you don't take."

– Wayne Gretzky

"It is never too late to be what
you might have been."

– George Eliot

"A person who never made
a mistake never tried
anything new."

– Albert Einstein

"The person who says it cannot be done should not interrupt the person who is doing it."
– Chinese Proverb

"Great minds discuss ideas;
average minds discuss events;
small minds discuss people."

– Eleanor Roosevelt

"You only live once,
but if you do it right,
once is enough."

– Mae West

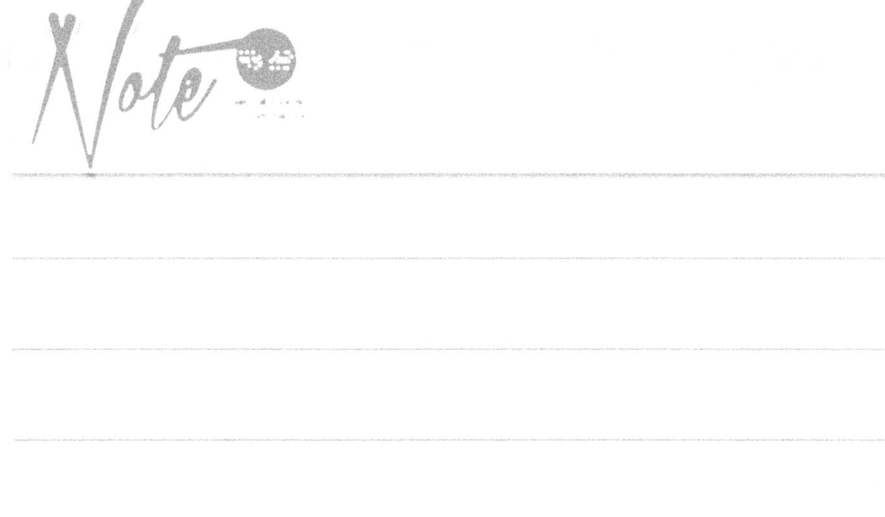

"If you tell the truth,
you don't have to remember
anything."

– Mark Twain

"The only thing worse
than being blind is having
sight but no vision."

– Helen Keller

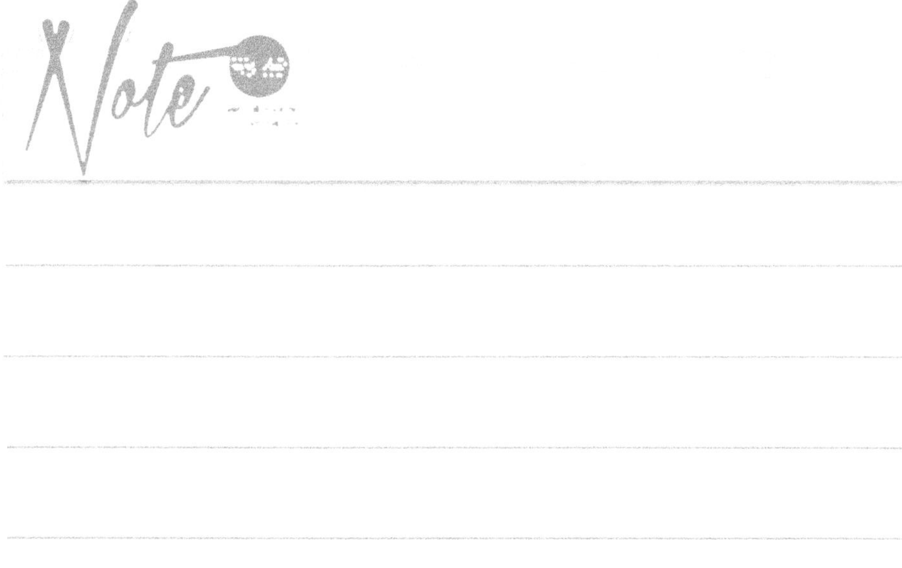

"To live is the rarest thing
in the world.
Most people exist, that is all."

– Oscar Wilde

Darkness cannot drive out darkness; only light can do that. Hate cannot drive out hate; only love can do that."
– **Martin Luther King, Jr**.

"The only thing we have to fear is fear itself."

– Franklin D. Roosevelt

"If you look at what you have in life, you'll always have more. If you look at what you don't have in life, you'll never have enough."

– Oprah Winfrey

"Remember no one can make you feel inferior without your consent."

– Eleanor Roosevelt

"For every minute you are angry you lose sixty seconds of happiness."

– Ralph Waldo Emerson

"Being deeply loved by someone gives you strength, while loving someone deeply gives you courage."

– Lao Tzu

"There are two ways of spreading light: to be the candle or the mirror that reflects it."

– Edith Wharton

"The road to success and the road to failure are almost exactly the same."

– Colin R. Davis

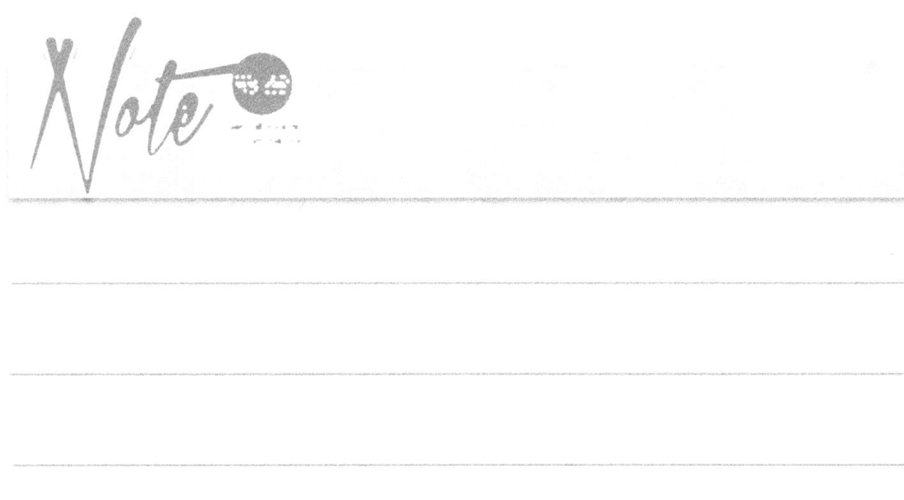

"Motivation is a fire from within. If someone else tries to light that fire under you, chances are it will burn very briefly."

– Stephen R. Covey

"In three words I can sum up
everything I've learned
about life:
It goes on."

– Robert Frost

"Self-reverence, self-knowledge, self control — these three alone lead to power."

– Alfred, Lord Tennyson

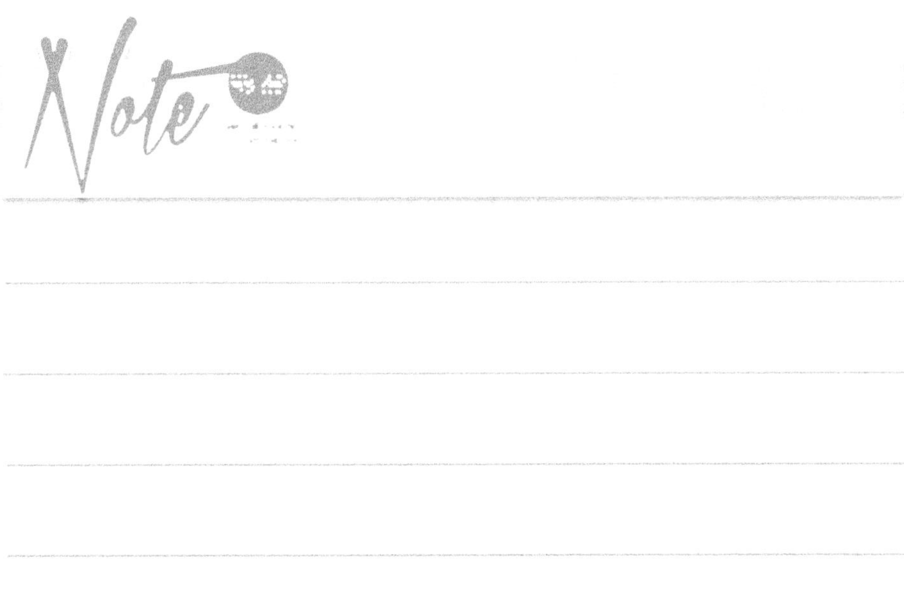

"Though no one can go back and make a brand new start, anyone can start from now and make a brand new ending."

– Carl Bard

"Anyone who stops learning is old, whether at twenty or eighty. Anyone who keeps learning stays young. The greatest thing in life is to keep your mind young."
– Henry Ford

"He who angers you conquers you."

– Elizabeth Kenny

"Beauty, without expression, tires."

– Ralph Waldo Emerson

"The secret of business is to know something that nobody else knows."

– Aristotle Onassis

"The greatest discovery of all time is that a person can change his future by merely changing his attitude."

– Oprah Winfrey

"We cannot always build
the future of our youth,
but we can build our youth
for the future."

– Franklin D. Roosevelt

"It takes courage to grow up and turn out to be who you really are."

– E.E. Cummings

"A man who views the world the same at 50 as he did at 20 has wasted 30 years of his life."

– Muhammad Ali

"In this world nothing can be said to be certain, except death and taxes."

– Benjamin Franklin

It is the mark of an educated
mind to be able to entertain
a thought without
accepting it."

– Aristotle

"A happy family is but an earlier heaven."

– George Bernard Shaw

"Don't walk in front of me,
I may not follow. Don't walk
behind me, I may not lead.
Walk beside me and be my
friend."

– Albert Camus

"Service to others is the rent
you pay for your room here
on earth."

– **Muhammad Ali**

"Courage doesn't always roar. Sometimes courage is the little voice at the end of the day that says 'I'll try again tomorrow.'"

– Mary Anne Radmacher

"Education is like a double-edged sword. It may be turned to dangerous uses if it is not properly handled."

– Wu Ting-Fang

Walking with a friend in the dark is better than walking alone in the light."

– Helen Keller

"Happiness is not a goal;
it is a by-product."

– Eleanor Roosevelt

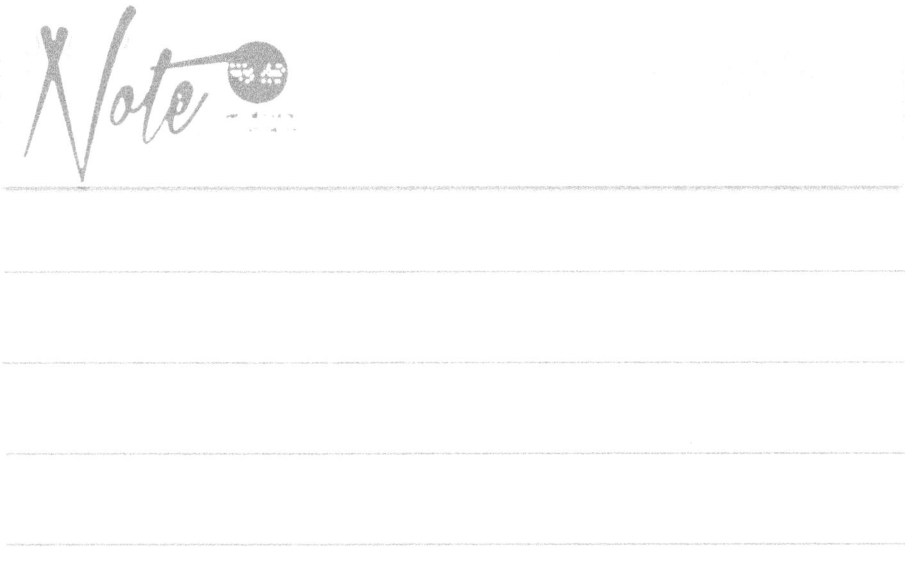

"Always forgive your enemies;
nothing annoys them so much."

– Oscar Wilde

"The only true wisdom is knowing that you know nothing."

– Socrates

"As a well-spent day brings happy sleep, so a life well spent brings happy death."

– Leonardo da Vinci

"Courage is what it takes to stand up and speak. Courage is also what it takes to sit down and listen."

– Winston Churchill

"Children are our most valuable resource."

– Herbert Hoover

"Love is, above all else, the gift of oneself."

– Jean Anouilh

"Music in the soul can be heard
by the universe."

– Lao Tzu

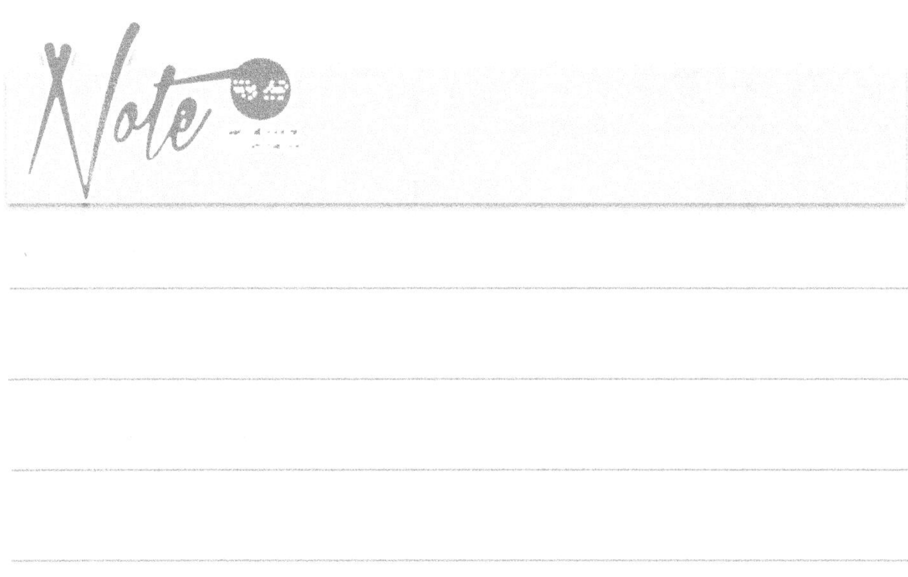

"Peace begins with a smile."

– Mother Teresa

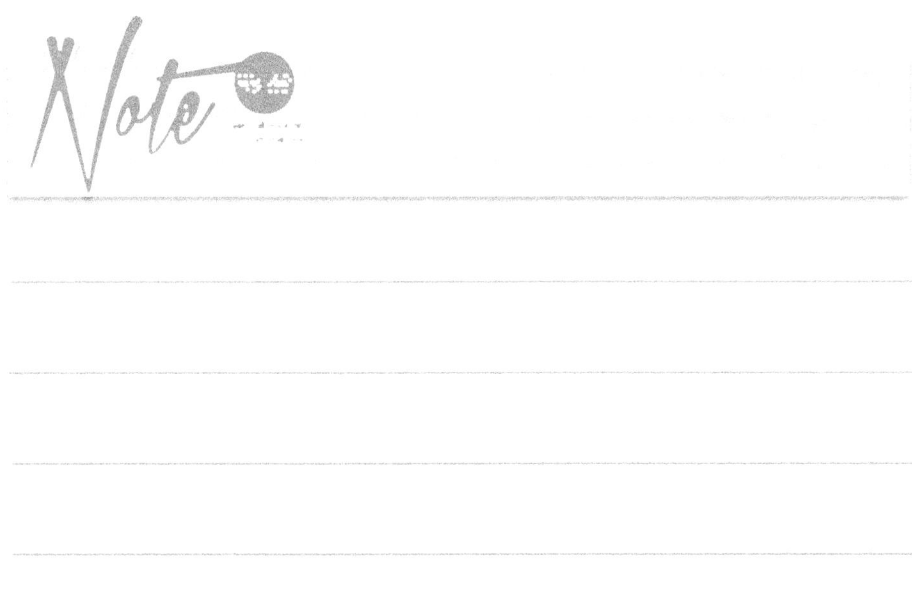

"Success is liking yourself,
liking what you do, and
liking how you do it."

– Maya Angelou

"A friend is someone who knows all about you and still loves you."

– Elbert Hubbard

"Never leave that till tomorrow which you can do today."

– Benjamin Franklin

"If you don't make mistakes, you're not working on hard enough problems."

– Frank Wilczek

"We must learn to live together as brothers or perish together as fools."

– Martin Luther King, Jr.

"Life is like a camera.
Just focus on what's important,
capture the good times, develop
from the negatives, and if things
don't work out, just take another
shot."

– Unknown

"When you judge another, you
do not define them;
you define yourself."

– Wayne Dyer

"He who is not courageous enough to take risks will accomplish nothing in life."

– Muhammad Ali

"Opportunity is missed by most people because it is dressed in overalls and looks like work."

– Thomas Edison

"Love me when I least deserve it, because that's when I really need it."

– Swedish Proverb

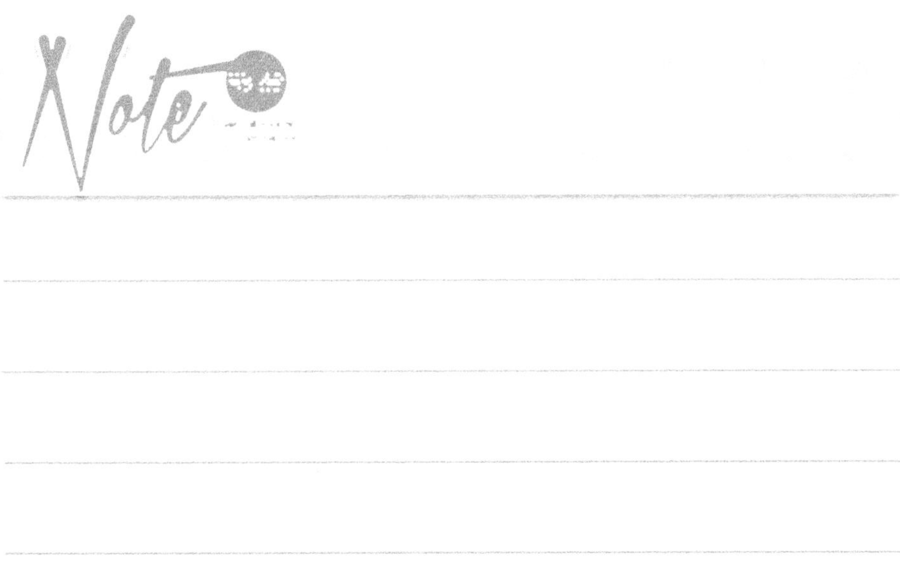

"The best and most beautiful things in the world cannot be seen or even touched.
They must be felt with the heart."

– Helen Keller

"If you want to test your memory, try to recall what you were worrying about one year ago today."

– E. Joseph Cossman

"The real opportunity for success lies within the person and not in the job."

– Zig Ziglar

"It takes a great deal of courage to stand up to your enemies, but even more to stand up to your friends."

– J. K. Rowling

Defeat is not bitter unless you swallow it."

– Joe Clark

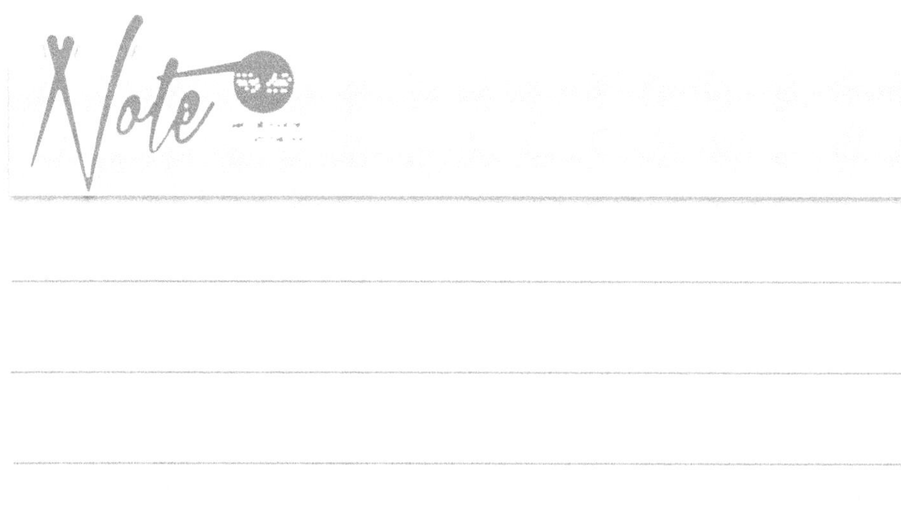

"A mind is like a parachute.
It doesn't work if it isn't open."

– Frank Zappa

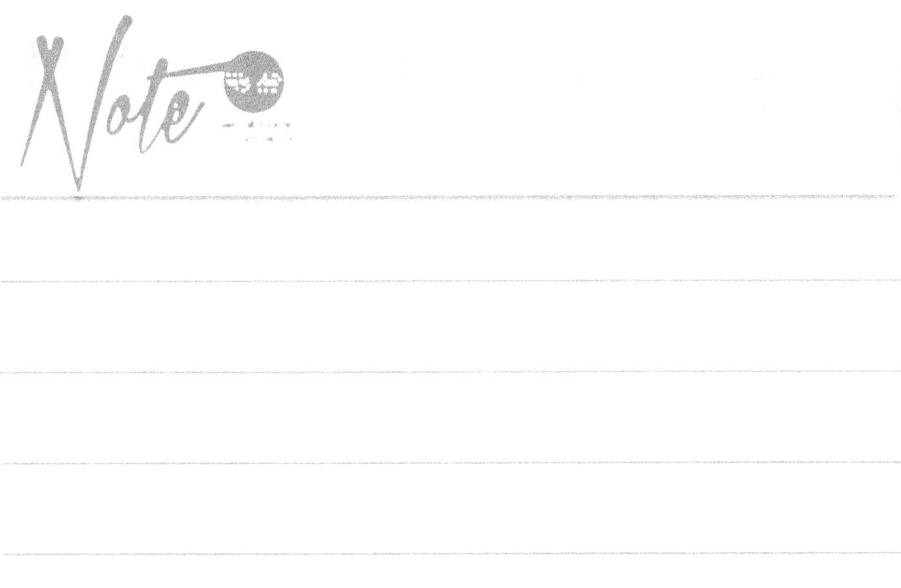

"Peace comes from within.
Do not seek it without."

– Muhammad Ali

"The man who removes a mountain begins by carrying away small stones."

– Chinese Proverbs

"When you are totally
at peace with yourself,
nothing can shake you."

– Deepam Chatterjee

"Be a first rate version of yourself, not a second rate version of someone else."

– Judy Garland

"Your worth consists
in what you are
and not in what you have."

– Thomas Edison

"Others can stop you temporarily
you are the only one
who can do it permanently."

– Zig Ziglar

"Life has no limitations,
except the ones you make."

– Les Brown

It's not bragging
if you can back it up."

– **Muhammad Ali**

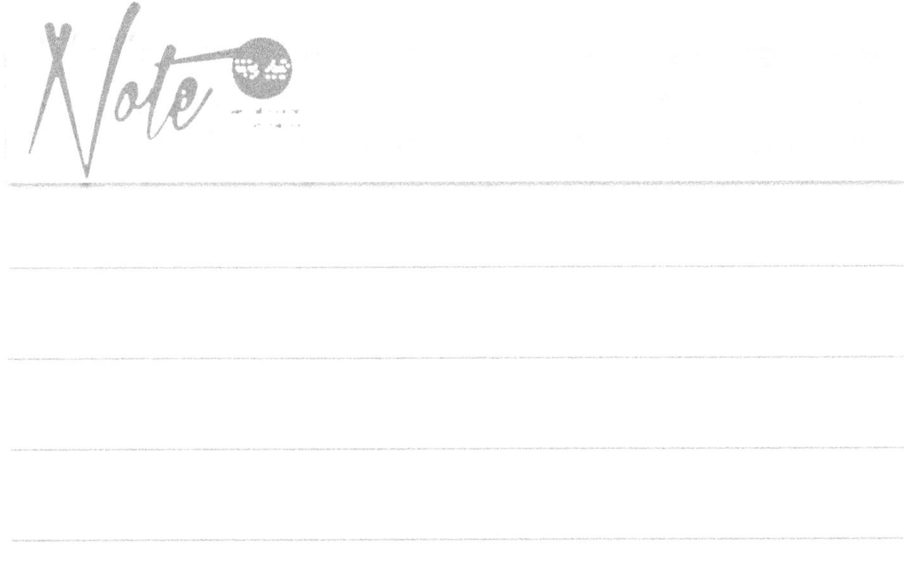

I love you the more in that
I believe you had liked me
for my own sake and for
nothing else.

– John Keats

But man is not made for defeat.
A man can be destroyed
but not defeated.

– Ernest Hemingway

When you reach the end
of your rope, tie a knot in it
and hang on.

– Franklin D. Roosevelt

There is nothing
permanent except change.

– Heraclitus.

You cannot shake hands
with a clenched fist.

– Indira Gandhi

Let us sacrifice our today
so that our children
can have a better tomorrow.

– A. P. J. Abdul Kalam

Do not mind anything that
anyone tells you
about anyone else.
Judge everyone and
everything for yourself.

– Henry James

9 7 9 8 6 3 7 5 0 3 8 4 1